Sugar, honey, ice & tea

by

C. R. Elliott

ISBN: 978-1089446873

for all of the broken hearted,

the beaten down

and the mistreated;

✝

the light resides within,

next to hope & strength

✝

may you find your way among the dark
and unsteady waters that you thread

CONTENT

C. R. ELLIOTT

the fragile

I was a flower,
with my feet steadily in the ground.
you're the water that gives me life.
take it away and and I start to wither.

- C. R. Elliott

you smell like trouble,
of mystery and risk.
is it possible to play with fire
without getting burned?

- C. R. Elliott

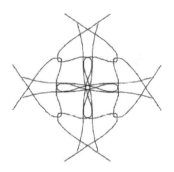

I need something to hold on,
a dream or a lie.
something to tell me what I'm doing wrong,
something to make me strong.

- C. R. Elliott

tears don't dry in here,
cause I am just a fool who believes in what
is lost.
my heart will carry on
as long as you wear that perfect smile on
your face.

can you hear me calling out your name?
in a night so quiet, I'm calling out in vain.
can you see me reaching out for you?
what a shame when I'm reaching what
can't come true

- C. R. Elliott

I am not affraid
to say *"i love you"*,
but I am scared to death
to fall in love with you

- C. R. Elliott

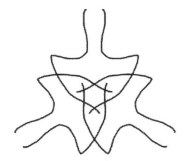

why can't it be so simple,
that what I have in my heart
I could hold in my hands

- C. R. Elliott

I am not addicted to you.
      you are not my drugs or alcohol.
you are my escape from reality.
      that is my addiction.

- C. R. Elliott

some days I stand here
in this body
and I do not feel at home.

- C. R. Elliott

just imagine,
being loved
the same as you give.

imagine.

- C. R. Elliott

there is nothing to lose
when no one knows your name.
what can I do
so things don't stay the same?
I am not playing this game
it gives no pleasure, only pain.

- C. R. Elliott

you gave me my best memories.
promise you will never become one.

- C. R. Elliott

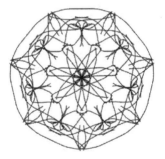

who would have thought
that a simple look
in your eyes
could fill my heart
with such joy

- C. R. Elliott

we used to knock
down walls together.
now it seems like
you are closing them in.
the same air that
used to give me life
has now become stale
and I am longing
to take a breath again.

- C. R. Elliott

you were the magic
that was missing from my life

- C. R. Elliott

we used to grow together,
now we just grow apart.
I pray for us to be happy,
but also pray for me to be free.

- C. R. Elliott

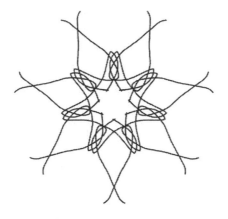

the sharpest heartache that hurts
is the love that stops
for no reason

- C. R. Elliott

I have lost myself
deep down inside.
in the shallow emptiness.
a place where my demons reside.

- C. R. Elliott

you were poison,
the sweet touch on my lips.
blackened my surrounding
addicted to your kiss.

- C. R. Elliott

the thought of you calms me down,
places my feet on the ground.
and if they make you happy,
that's fine by me.
I am broken inside
but that you will never see.

- C. R. Elliott

my heart is just too tired to care.
who do you call
when there is no one there?

- C. R. Elliott

you got yourself
a new light,
but I am still invisible
for you can't see me in the dark

- C. R. Elliott

my heart was thrown
in mysterious places
from which it is too dark
to fight the current
and find my way back home

- C. R. Elliott

hold me close in the dead of night,
as I can't be alone tonight.
all these demons holding me tight
from all the weight inside my mind.
you're the stars shining bright
making my heart find the light.

- C. R. Elliott

can you hear me
echoing all through the night?
can you hear me
breaking on this muted sky?

- C. R. Elliott

I dreamt
of all the things that we could,
and awakened
from all the things that we could not

- C. R. Elliott

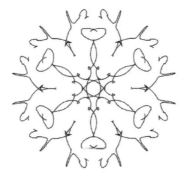

let our lips tell the stories
how our hearts really feel

- C. R. Elliott

in a perfect world
        my heartache would not exist.
in a perfect world
        my soul would be fixed.

- C. R. Elliott

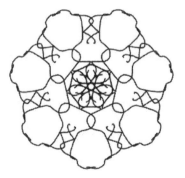

it hurts even more
knowing it is over,
than the times I
knew
we were heading
there

- C. R. Elliott

you asked why does it hurt.

I whispered,

"because it was real"

- C. R. Elliott

the kiss of dawn
shows all the beauty.
the dead of night
hides it away.
the world can light the sparks
around us
that our eyes would never find
if the heart is blind.

- C. R. Elliott

I am a boat stranded at see.
I let things go
so the current can carry me.

- C. R. Elliott

I still remember the
colour of your eyes,
even if the rest escapes me

- C. R. Elliott

sometimes I stare out my window at night,
gazing at the moon,
wondering if its beautiful light
reaches you too.

\- C. R. Elliott

darling,

you do not fear love,
you fear of loving **wrong**

- C. R. Elliott

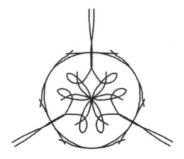

do not hide from pain.
in darkness,
where shadows can't be seen,
it is easy,
but you need light to survive

- C. R. Elliott

the fall

you were the light behind my eyes.
but like the sun goes down every day
for the moon to take its place,
you took that light
and cast me in the dark.

\- C. R. Elliott

I am one stitch away from making it
and one scar away from falling apart.

- C. R. Elliott

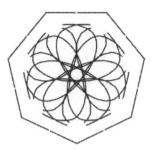

I was a flower on your window stand,
with my feet steady in the ground.
I took life from the water you gave.

soon your visits started to be rear.
left me in the burning sun in despair.
broken and thirsty I still wanted you near,
my heart of lonely and full of fear
that one day will come
for me to disappear.

- C. R. Elliott

feels like I'm rusting away
slowly every day.
turn into a shadow of myself.
from inside I decay.

reach out and pull me in
for you are the reason I started living
and the reason I started to fade.
each day a differnt struggle,
even on sunny days
there's a cloud over me.

drenched in rain,
drowning in my pain.
but you can't see me cry,
from all the tears in my eye.
poured onto the ground
I fall without making a sound.

- C. R. Elliott

my life is now nothing
but a shallow echo
in a puddle below my feet

- C. R. Elliott

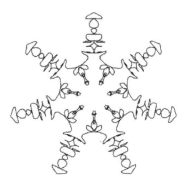

as I stand here
with tears in my eye,
I still remember
the good times
before we said goodbye

- C. R. Elliott

when they take away
the very thing that fills your **heart**
you see just how **empty**
this world can truly get

- C. R. Elliott

I know you only hurt me
to distract from your pain.
the worse thing is
that I am letting you.

- C. R. Elliott

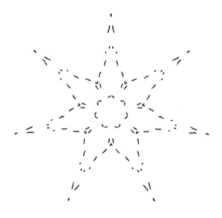

you were the venom
that chilled my heart
and burned my soul.
and somehow,
I am still addicted
to your touch

- C. R. Elliott

why am I still holding on
to dreams that are
better left to fray
and carried by the wind,
because I know
I am much better
if they go away?

- C. R. Elliott

the look in your eyes
and the crack in your voice
sends shivers down my spine
and my heart into spiral,
for I am lost to know
how to help you

- C. R. Elliott

and maybe, my dear
we were nothing but a dream
and it is best we stay that way

- C. R. Elliott

we had a wonderful
story.
wish that the ending
could be the same.

- C. R. Elliott

you can speak the words of love
in many languages,
just not the one that really matters–
coming from the heart

- C. R. Elliott

I have been lost for ages.
I don't know
who I am anymore.
is this a dream
or a faded memory?

- C. R. Elliott

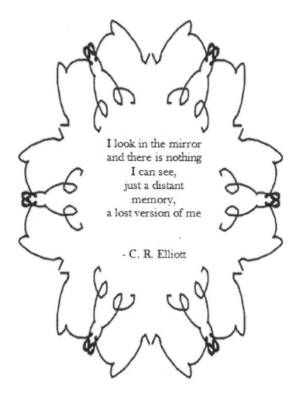

I look in the mirror
and there is nothing
I can see,
just a distant
memory,
a lost version of me

- C. R. Elliott

the last thing I wanted
was for you to lose you place,
to leave your heart in debt
just to make me happy

- C. R. Elliott

I opened up
and gave you my heart.
how foolish love can be
to give up all control.

- C. R. Elliott

one of these days
the sky is going to break
and reveal to the world
all your past mistakes.

- C. R. Elliott

I am standing on the edge of reason,
trying to find my own.
trying to find a new beginning,
a place to call my own.

- C. R. Elliott

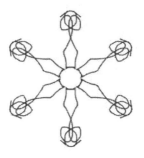

I am living in my past delusions.
fighting for another try.
fighting for another chance,
to make things right.

- C. R. Elliott

I am here

with a beautiful soul,
while you are looking
for a beautiful face

- C. R. Elliott

how many sleepless nights
must I endure?
how many heartbreaks
must I survive
for you to finally realise,
to stop and see,
that it is wrong
the way you are treating me?

- C. R. Elliott

my heart is at war
    from your silence
        that cuts deep like violence

- C. R. Elliott

I always leave pieces
wherever I go,
giving away parts of my soul,
no wonder I don't feel whole

- C. R. Elliott

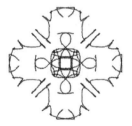

I drifted so far away
I started to detach.
how can I know
I am still going the right way
if I am not the same person
when I started?

- C. R. Elliott

of all the paths that I could walk
I chose the one that lead me to you

- C. R. Elliott

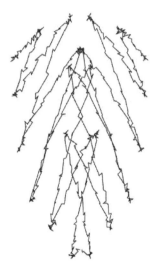

life is the only road we walk
that does not have warning signs
along the way

- C. R. Elliott

how can it be so easy for you
to tell me you *love me*
while holding someone else

- C. R. Elliott

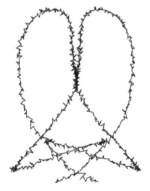

from mountains high
to oceans deep.
my love knows no limits
when it comes to you.

- C. R. Elliott

when the storm passes
we can still smell the rain.
I am a rainbow
painted through the sky,
made by the memories
of your goodbye.

- C. R. Elliott

my heart is broken
and thrown into abyss.
not from the lies or pain,
but from your thought
thinking my love was just a game.

- C. R. Elliott

I don't regret loving you.
I regret loving you that much.
I regret loving you that long.

- C. R. Elliott

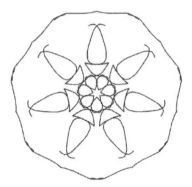

I have been in the dark
for far too long
to settle for a candle.
it is fun when I can see,
but I need a proper light
to shine on me.

- C. R. Elliott

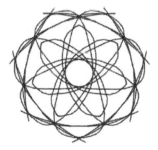

the brink of dawn
cuts like a razor.
all the beauty
escapes my eyes
from the words
of a dreaded betrayal.
so I wait and run
to hide from the sun.

- C. R. Elliott

did you ever wonder,
just how much I cared,
that I broke all my rules for you?

- C. R. Elliott

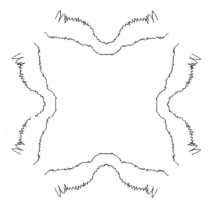

I hope the day never comes
for you to wake up empty,
realizing just how much of you
I have filled.

- C. R. Elliott

you ignited the fire in my heart.
watched it burn right from the start.
when you saw the flames started to recede,
you stepped aside
and left me to bleed.
as the smoke cleared
it was obvious to see
that there was nothing left of me.

- C. R. Elliott

we ache for flying among the clouds,
not knowing it comes with a fall

- C. R. Elliott

you tore me down to pieces,
just to watch me beg for love

- C. R. Elliott

I keep on wishing
for someone to take me away.
away from this wasted life
I have been living.
to find me a way
to leave it all behind.
to hide from the pain
that cripples my bones.
a place I can make my own.
a place I can call a home.
it would be so easy to let go,
but I don't want to walk away.
I just need some shelter
so my mind doesn't start to fray.

- C. R. Elliott

C. R. ELLIOTT

the strength

I want to be naked with you,
so our souls touch and twine.
I want to show you my emotions.
I want to tell you my wildest dreams
and my deepest secrets.
to share with you
as you would share with me.
I want to be naked with you
I want my soul to be free.

- C. R. Elliott

the strongest are those who cry in pain.
living their life in shame,
but never show they are broken,
from all the words left unspoken.
‡
we are the ones who carry on.
the ones who pick up the pieces,
when everyone has left.
the ones that put ourselves together
in the dark
day by day,
but in the end go right back to the start.
‡
we continue to make ourselves whole.
so we can smile during the day
and pretend we are alright,
but the truth is we're dying inside.

- C. R. Elliott

like the fall of the tide
I need to step back
in order to collect myself again

- C. R. Elliott

you think my scars make me weaker,
but they make me stronger.
every one of them has a story and holds a
name.
they remind me that the past is real
and that the future won't be the same.

- C. R. Elliott

I will finally see
how much you helped me
   when you become
   a bittersweet past tense

     - C. R. Elliott

I don't blame you
for breaking my heart,
        nor for all the tears I have cried.
        I blame you for not giving me time
to fall out of love with you,
before tearing me apart.

- C. R. Elliott

don't fool yourself.

family does not necessarily mean home.
home is not a place,
not even a person.
home is a feeling.
a feeling of love,
where support and warmth are given.
if there is a lack of those,
then family is not a home,
it is a cage with familiar faces.

- C. R. Elliott

how messed up it must be,
for me to run away
from the things I should run too?

- C. R. Elliott

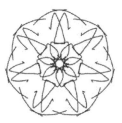

I wear my smile like a mask
for the whole world to see.
it cuts deep
but I want it to hurt only for me

- C. R. Elliott

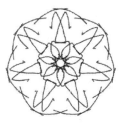

there is a fire inside me
that will never go out.
so try to break down my door,
but the rest of the fortress
will still stand.

- C. R. Elliott

it scares me how much you changed,

but then I remember,

the devil was once an angel too

- C. R. Elliott

music is my escape
        when life becomes a nightmare

- C. R. Elliott

I said I don't want to forget;

then you whispered,

"you can't forget what is always there"

- C. R. Elliott

nothing ever felt
so much
like home
as being buried
deep in your arms

- C. R. Elliott

it's dangerous
being alone for so long.
it makes you so strong.

- C. R. Elliott

knowing how to love ourselves
    is the first love we need to learn

- C. R. Elliott

every autumn the leaves fall
and every spring they bloom again.
so why would you think I can't do the
same?

- C. R. Elliott

do not underestimate
what you don't understand,
for I am like water,
kind to give you life
and strong enough to drown
if the current turns.

- C. R. Elliott

it is ironic how our hearts
      can still keep on beating
            even after they are broken

- C. R. Elliott

it never felt so good being lost
as it did when I swam
in the ocean
that is your eyes

- C. R. Elliott

don't be afraid of the dark
just because the moon
has a different glow
than the sun

- C. R. Elliott

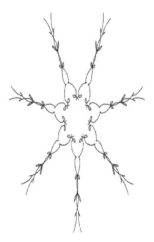

listen to your heart,
for it knows which
love will hold you
and which love
will hold you back

- C. R. Elliott

be careful how you play.
    if you break me
I will put myself back
    like a puzzle.
it just might be
    a different picture.

\- C. R. Elliott

when you thread that road
covered with thorns,
I will be there
to greet you with a smile

- C. R. Elliott

plant your seed
everywhere you go.
sprinkle it around
and watch the flowers grow.
we are only as good
as the love that we give.
make sure yours is warm
so you see them bloom.

- C. R. Elliott

don't let them dim your flame
just so you can fit in.
I rather stand alone
then in a crowd
where I am half lit.

- C. R. Elliott

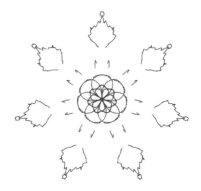

every rose
needs a little rain
if it wants to grow

- C. R. Elliott

when alone, just remember,
the moon is up there too,
watching over you,

always

- C. R. Elliott

the most *broken* **smiles**
have the **prettiest** *hearts*

- C. R. Elliott

open wounds are finally healing
from words without meaning.
spoken with hurtful intent
for my heart on the mend.

- C. R. Elliott

all is lost and gone away,
there is nothing left to say.
all these memories that remain,
my hopes and dreams were all in vain.
I still wonder what I will do,
as a small part of me is still in love with you.
we can't play this foolish game anymore,
one of us has to walk out the door.
It is a small price to pay
to make you fade away.

- C. R. Elliott

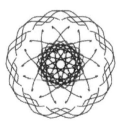

a bird needs the open sky
to spread its wings
if it wants to fly.
don't settle for a place
that doesn't give you room to grow.

- C. R. Elliott

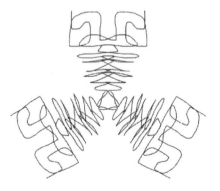

the truth is that I am stronger than you think.
I just put things aside
so we would not sink.

- C. R. Elliott

I am not going to shield you
from the truth.
I care too much
to speak beautiful lies to you.
even if it hurts
I will be right here
to pick you from the dirt.

- C. R. Elliott

as painful as it is,
hearts must sometimes break
in order to make a better
shape.

- C. R. Elliott

love will come
      when your heart is ready
           to carry it

- C. R. Elliott

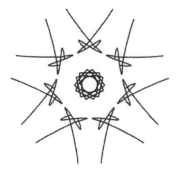

I can fill a whole ocean
with my tears.
that way
I never have to be alone.

- C. R. Elliott

we should not be ashamed of our **scars,**
for they are the ones,
that truly **healed** us

- C. R. Elliott

when you're walking on clouds,
watch where you place you feet.
you look down on us in smile
and I know everything will be alright,
because when you are in my heart
you are never truly gone.

- C. R. Elliott

I guess it is easy for you to
say,
but guess what honey,
it is not that good for me

- C. R. Elliott

fears are anchors
that bring us down.
if we want to float
we must break the chains
so we can be free

- C. R. Elliott

C. R. ELLIOTT

the rise

how can I breath from this air
that is killing me?
suffocating in this hell I am in.

I am stronger than this.
I will prevail.
because nor the nightmare around me
and the hell beneath me
can not break me
and take me for what I truly am.

free

- C. R. Elliott

you can have my heart
but you're not in control.
I give you my time
but you don't say where I go.
you can have my all
but my identity is not for sale.

- C. R. Elliott

and I still wonder,
how can someone so beautiful
be so miserable

- C. R. Elliott

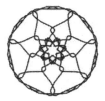

the reflection in the mirror is me,
how you treat me is how you see.

*am **I broken** or am **I free***?

- C. R. Elliott

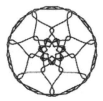

even the harshest words
and the deepest wounds
will one day heal.
shattered reflection will remain
and I will never be the same.

thank you for proving my worth.

- C. R. Elliott

I always say *"sorry"*,
even if I am not in the wrong.
my love is just greater
than my ego.

- C. R. Elliott

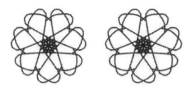

the ocean doesn't apologise
for its depth.
the mountain doesn't apologise
for the space it takes.
the wind doesn't apologise
for its strength
and neither will I!

- C. R. Elliott

once you lose me
and try to get me back,
just know that I am not the same person.

- C. R. Elliott

even when the earth

falls out of balance

the light will always be there to find you

- C. R. Elliott

you look for love with your eyes.
if you would look with your heart
into mine
it would never stop craving.

- C. R. Elliott

mistreat me.
that is the easiest way
to learn just how easy
life can be without you.

- C. R. Elliott

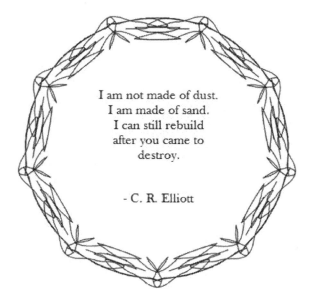

I am not made of dust.
I am made of sand.
I can still rebuild
after you came to
destroy.

- C. R. Elliott

there will come a day
when I will forget
        the colour of your eyes,
the day my heart will start to heal
        and be alright.
but I will still remember
how you made me feel.

    like a dream. a distant memory.

- C. R. Elliott

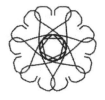

every time you touch
I get hurt.
like thorns from a rose,
hold me gentle when you're close.

- C. R. Elliott

this is the last fight,
the last breath
I am wasting on you.
the last time
you will break my spirit in two.

- C. R. Elliott

I still remember the **good times**
     when life was but a dream.
but I also know
   how much better I am **without you**.

- C. R. Elliott

why can't we see
that words are deceiving?
they don't mean a thing.
all they do is bring you harm,
for strength and hope to disarm.

- C. R. Elliott

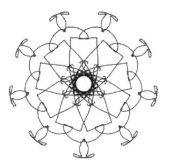

took me countless tears to see,
you were not the one for me.
all this shame I had to hide,
saying that I was fine
while my heart beated out of line.
guess that was just a lie
to bring back some hope in my eye.

- C. R. Elliott

thank you *LIFE*
for teaching me
all the things
I never
wanted to learn

- C. R. Elliott

it does not matter where you are planted
or what you are made of.
all that matters is that you bloom.

- C. R. Elliott

every grain of sand has a story.
every star has a name.
I am my own.

Unique

- C. R. Elliott

what a silly world
        you must live in,
        to expect me to give you my all
with nothing in return.

- C. R. Elliott

as the day turns into dark,
that's how easy it was
for you to tear me apart.
don't think I'll be here for long
as the light in me is too strong.
soon I'll be the sun
that rises above the clouds.
and honey, trust me when I say,
my bright light
won't cast a shadow.

- C. R. Elliott

the light can not reach me
if the sun is covered by the clouds.
sometimes we need to step aside
in order for us to have the space to grow.

- C. R. Elliott

fine,
kill me if you must,
it will just give you
a new me

- C. R. Elliott

the brightest hour
of our darkest day
truly is,
when the true colours of people
finally start to appear

- C. R. Elliott

your love can make me bleed,
but I will never plead for it

- C. R. Elliott

I have seen too many sunsets
to ever doubt
how beautiful endings
can really be

- C. R. Elliott

you may tear down my roof,
but the foundations are still standing.

I am a rebuild home
risen from the wreckage.
I am locking the door
and leaving you out in the cold.

\- C. R. Elliott

I always walk with my shadow behind me.
if the sun turns,
then so do I.
I do not walk away from the light
just to be in the dark.

- C. R. Elliott

there is no such thing as perfect.
we all have our flaws
and we all made mistakes.
we are not perfect.

*we are **unique***

- C. R. Elliott

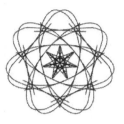

the moon has its phases
and so do I.
I am still shining bright
whether I am
half or full

- C. R. Elliott

I love you,

for finding beauty in my negative spaces

- C. R. Elliott

tore your pictures
from the wall.
set them down
and burn them all.
all the memories
go up in smoke,
the image of you now
nothing but a ghost.
it seems right
to end with fire
as that is how
it began.

- C. R. Elliott

the true meaning of understanding
is to know
not all things are meant to be understood

- C. R. Elliot

if you don't find comfort
and accept who you are,
you will never feel at home

- C. R. Elliott

first,
learn to love yourself,
<u>then watch others follow</u>

- C. R. Elliott

struggle makes you bloom a flower.
honey, believe me when I say,
some have the most beautiful gardens.

- C. R. Elliott

I look for scars.
not to cut them deeper,
but because I know
how it is to be broken
and I want to make them heal.

- C. R. Elliott

endings are not always bad –

the most beautiful of colours
are seen on the horizon,
where the day kisses the night
goodbye

- C. R. Elliott

EPILOGUE

Thank you for coming this far –

the end,

with my heart in your hands, gently wrapped
around your fingers as you turned the pages
made from tears and pain, poured out on
paper in ink.

Hope you found some solace in the lines
writen in between these pages as I did while
writing them.

Life is made of bitter and sweet,
but we are all made out of:

sugar, honey, ice & tea

C. R. Elliott

Made in the USA
San Bernardino, CA
06 January 2020